Credit Score Repair 101

The only credit score guide that you will ever need

AMARPREET SINGH

Publisher - The Thought Flame

THE THOUGHT FLAME
TURNING SPARK INTO FLAME

info@thethoughtflame.com

www.thethoughtflame.com

Table of Contents

Introduction

I want to thank you and congratulate you for downloading the book, *"Credit Score Repair 101: The Only Credit Score Repair Guide That You Will Ever Need."*

We all know how important your credit rating is and what it can hold for your future endeavors. Whether you are looking for a way to improve your credit score so that you can eventually get a new car, apply for a mortgage for a new hours or simply want to place yourself in a much better position for the future, this is certainly the book that you want to read today.

When it comes to finding a way to get all of your finances back on track, it is extremely important to take your overall credit rating into account. This book will offer you a variety of different ways that you can improve your credit today as well as a few proven tips that will have your credit rating shooting back up to an acceptable rating in no time.

Thank you again for downloading this eBook. I hope that you thoroughly enjoy it!

Chapter One: Why Is Your Credit So Important?

Your credit rating is an important aspect of your financial health. Your credit rating is also dubbed as your credit score or your creditworthiness. An individual's credit score ranges from 300 as the least favorable score to 850 as the most favorable score. Your actions affect your credit rating but the assessment of credit score is done by a credit reference agency. This rating implies your capability to pay for debts and other expenditures. That is why it is used primarily for loan and credit applications. Aside from the score, a credit report will contain other information. This information may be used for other lawful purposes as well.

Different individuals or institutions ask for your credit report for various reasons. As a matter of fact, there are some employers who ask for this information. If you have a bad record, be it financially or not, it might show up on the credit report. In case you have a record, the employer would either think twice about hiring you or disregard your application in an instant.

Ultimately your credit score reflects your reputation built from your transactions with lenders, banks, and other financial institutions. These transactions comprise your credit history. The higher the score, the more reputable you are. If you have a good reputation, then lenders would be more than willing to offer you great loan options. On the other hand, you are left with limited loan options and the process would be harder if your reputation is not that good. In worst cases, there are applicants with unfavorable credit rating who are denied of their credit or loan applications.

Aside from standard lenders, banks also look at the credit scores of the individuals who want to open accounts, most especially those who are applying for credit cards. Credit card abuse is deemed the main reason for the low credit score of an individual. The individual may not be paying his credit card dues on time or they may not be paying at all. Banks have to be cautioned about credit card abusers. That is why they ask the services of a credit reference agency to determine the credit history and credit rating of a person.

How To Tell When You Are Headed For Financial Trouble Immediately

The truth is: many people don't realize that they are heading into financial ruin until it is too late. Often, telltale signs of potentially disastrous situations are ignored, with the mistaken belief that these money-related problems would eventually blow over and that there won't be any damaging repercussions in the long run.

Unfortunately, ignoring such situations will not only lower your credit score, but it will also make it harder to regain financial stability afterwards, especially in terms of rebuilding bank savings, asking for future loans, and having enough cash on hand.

In this section I want to teach you the top five signs that you are headed for financial debt so you can recognize them at once and put a stop to them before anything gets out of hand.

1. Misusing Your Credit Cards

While using your credit card is not necessarily a bad thing, it can become bad once you start relying on it for all your spending without any thought to its corresponding interest rates or service charges and without any kind of regard for the payment that you have to make later on. If this is something that you are doing now then you are already walking on shaky financial ground.

Your credit cards should only be used when absolutely necessary, and not for the sake of convenience. If possible, use cash whenever you can, especially for smaller and incidental expenditures to avoid racking up more debts.

2. Counting On Your Chickens Before The Eggs Have Even Hatched

You know that you are in serious financial trouble when you are banking on possible payoffs that have very little chances of materializing; examples of which include:

-Future birthday, graduation, wedding money gifts, etc.

-Potential inheritance

-Profits from a soon-to-be-launched business venture

If these payoffs do not push through, what would happen then?

3. Paying Off Your Debt Using Your Credit Cards

Many people simply sign up for debt consolidation for the sheer "convenience" of making one monthly payment to all their creditors. However, using this lending option while you still have available credit could greatly lower your credit score.

At the same time, debt consolidation can be considered as taking out a larger loan to pay off your smaller debts. This is an option that is best used when you don't have available credit to spare. Otherwise, you end up with a bigger loan that is 50% to 200% more than the combined amount of your smaller debts.

4. Paying All Of Your Credit Card Bills Late

Unable to regularly pay your bills on time is a clear indicator of your inability to manage your funds. Aside from destroying your financial credibility, this practice also saddles you with late fees that could easily amount to hundreds of dollars in one year.

The same is true when it comes to paying off a small percentage of your monthly bills just so you can keep using basic services (e.g. utilities, phone lines, etc.) Paying your bills on time and in full can help keep your credit score stable, and eliminate additional service fees.

5. Having One Too Many Credit Cards

All credit cards carry interest rates, finance charges, and other hidden fees as well. So if you have 2 active credit cards, you also need to pay off twice the interest rates, twice the service charges, and twice the miscellaneous fees ... per month. Now imagine if you have 5 active credit cards all at once...

I cannot stress enough how important your credit is. Take it from me, I was once in a position when my credit fell below 500 and it seemed that there was absolutely nothing I could do, from renting a simple 1 bedroom apartment to even going back to college. Your credit is your life and as such you need to take care of it as best as possible and take into account how crucial it is to your future.

Chapter Two: Five Ways To Begin Improving Your Credit Right Now

Regrettably, many people do not really pay too much attention to their credit ratings until they start having troubles with it. You might have realized that when you have a bad credit score, it is not just your ability to get an approved loan that gets affected but you will definitely have problems when you try to obtain any type of credit at all. If you previously enjoyed having store financing, that would stop. You will be required to pay deposits on your phone line and other utilities at home. You may even have troubles in renting a new property. If you are currently suffering from a bad credit, do not despair. There is hope for you.

All that you need to do is take the necessary actions for credit repair as soon as possible. In this chapter I will outline the five steps on how you can improve your credit standing right now before it is too late.

Step One: Get Your Credit Report

This first step is critical because your credit report will include all of the credit information conveyed by your banks and other credit institutions you owe money from. Your credit report holds the secret on how you can proceed with your credit repair process. A lot of people do not really think about getting a copy of their credit report unless they are faced with the hurdle of credit repair. But you need to understand that even when you have a credit standing, you will still need to regularly review your credit report to make sure that they do not contain any errors that can detrimentally affect your credit score.

Normally, you should not pay any charges to get a copy of your credit report. All you have to do is ask for it through a written request together with a photocopy of your valid ID. When you get a disapproval for a credit card or car loan application, ask the credit institution which of the credit bureaus reported your poor credit standing. Repairing your credit will start by taking meticulously reviewing your credit report to check if there are any inaccuracies.

If ever you noticed any errors or inaccuracies, you can send a letter to the credit bureaus to request them to look into the items that you dispute. Attaching documents such as payment receipts can make it easier for the credit bureaus to investigate your claim. Include as much details and information as you can so that the process of repairing your credit report can be done more quickly.

Step Two: Get In Touch With All Of Your Creditors

After you have carefully reviewed your credit report and found that there are no errors or inaccuracies, your next step in repairing your credit score is to contact the different credit institutions that you have delinquent debts with. Your success in repairing your credit standing can actually depend on how quickly you can work with your creditors in solving your problems.

In most instances, creditors usually treat the recovery of their money from their debtors as their first priority. A lot of people have actually been astonished upon learning that the creditors do accommodate requests for loan restructuring which can allow their debtors to have payment terms that are more reasonable for them. In certain cases, creditors can choose to reduce or even eliminate the interests charged on the unpaid balance. In other cases, creditors can even agree to lessen the principal balance itself if the debtors agree to make immediate payment of the full balance amount.

Always keep in mind that the primary objective in this exercise is to repair your credit standing. Make sure that you do not commit to any payment scheme with your creditors, which you think you are not capable of meeting. If you do so, you will only end up with much bigger problems that you started with. If you keep missing your monthly payments even after your creditor has given you the chance to come up with a better payment plan, your creditor may lose their trust in you and may no longer for another restructuring of your loans.

It is extremely important that you agree to a new payment scheme that is truly workable for you. When you do this, your credit standing will be repaired more quickly.

Step Three: Avoid Your Debt From Reaching Collection Agencies

When your creditors have finally determined that it is quite impossible to collect from you, they will be forced to sell your unpaid debt balances to collection agencies. This means that your creditors have decided that the possibility of collecting from you is so minimal that they are prepared to lose a portion of those unpaid loan amounts just to be able to collect something from you. Majority of debts sold to collection agencies are discounted for up to 50%, which means that your creditors will only be able to collect only half of what you owe them even if you make the full payment.

This is the worst possible thing that could happen to your credit and you will want to avoid it at all costs. When your creditors sell your unpaid loans to collection agencies, they have technically "written off" your loans in their books. When they do so, you will see that your credit report will receive the lowest possible rating from them. If you reach this lowest point in the credit cycle, it is advisable to take immediate actions to start your credit repair. When the collection agencies start calling you, they will force you to start paying your loans.

Before you allow yourself to be harassed by collection agents, it is much better if you can talk to your creditors first. Discuss your current financial situation with your creditors and ask if they can reverse the "write off" score from your credit history. Some creditors are willing to do this but they may require you to immediate pay your unpaid balance. The basic idea here is to look for all possible ways to move your unpaid loans from the collection agencies back in the books of your creditors.

If your creditor is no longer willing to negotiate with you, you will then have to work with the collection agencies. Collection agents normally employ collection tactics that aim to intimidate and threaten the debtors. They are also known for the usual threats of taking non-paying debtors to court if they remain unwilling to pay their unpaid loan balances. While dealing with collection agents, you need to always remember two things: first, the collection agency purchased your loan balance from the creditors for less than the actual unpaid amount and second, it is not likely that they will really take you to court for not paying your loan balance.

Your best option when dealing with collection agents is to offer to pay an amount as high as you can squeeze out of your budget to show them that you have the willingness to pay your debts if only your financial status will allow it.

Step Four: Apply For A Secured Credit Card of Your Choice

The process of repairing your credit standing can be a lengthy process. You may have to spend a couple of years to build your credit score back to an acceptable level. As we have mentioned earlier, credit, especially credit cards, have become an essential part of our modern lives. You really do not have to suffer with paying everything with cash while you are waiting for your credit to be repaired. You can always apply for a secured credit card, which is normally offered by credit card companies for people who have poor credit standing. Maybe you already know that when you have poor credit standing, it will be quite impossible for your applications for a regular credit card to be approved.

Secured credit cards are different from regular credit cards in such a way that you will have to provide an initial deposit that has an equal amount as the credit limit. Simply stated, if you want a credit limit of $ 1,000, you will have to make an initial deposit of $200 to as much as $1,000 before your application can be approved. You will then give the credit card company the right to credit your bank account in case you miss any of your monthly payments.

When you already have your own secured credit card, make sure that you use it very wisely. Make sure that you use it regularly but make sure that you only use it for basic necessities so you will be able to manage your monthly payments. When you are able to maintain prompt payments over a long period of time, you will be able to gradually repair your credit standing as you earn your creditor's trust in you.

Step Five: Get Help From Companies That Specialize In Credit Repair

If you are in far deeper trouble and the above steps do not seem to help your situation, you can think about seeking help from a company with specialization in credit repair. Of course, as expected, these companies will offer their services to "clean up your credit standing" in exchange for a fee.

Even though a lot of people have claimed that these credit repair companies have successfully helped them in their financial woes, you need to understand that those success stories may have different situations from yours. It is very important for you to be extra cautious when choosing a credit repair company because there are a lot of scammers out there. Before you even sign up for any credit repair services, you need to make sure that you understand all of the terms in the agreement, including fine print. In most instances, you can actually perform yourself whatever those credit card companies offer to do for you. Getting their services is actually ideal when you do not have the time to perform those necessary action steps or a detailed plan on how to do it.

Normally, the fundamental strategy that those credit repair companies employ is to persuade you to dispute with the credit bureaus almost all of the details reflected on your credit report. The premise is to flood the credit bureaus with as many requests as you can muster to prepare which they will find impossible to reply to within the 30-day window period.

Remember what we mentioned earlier, if the credit bureaus will not be able to respond to your requests within the window period, they will be obliged to take out of your credit report whatever details you are disputing. But a lot of people have really questioned this particular strategy because even though the credit bureaus are obliged to remove any of the items that you dispute, they will carry on with their investigation of your claims. In case they ultimately find out that there is no basis for your claims, they will just add those details back on your credit report again. So it will just be a vicious cycle.

It is also a good idea to compare different credit repair companies first before signing up. This way, you will be able to see which of them can provide the best service for your particular situation.

While this may seem like a hassle at first, trust me you will not regret it later. The moment you begin to see yourself facing future financial troubles, get the help you need immediately. As long as you follow the steps outlined in this chapter, you should be able to avoid trouble immediately and improve your credit score before it gets worse.

Chapter Three: How To Get Rid Of Your Bad Credit and Build Credit At The Same

We all want to build good credit – it's important to do so because it is an essential part of life. It not only helps us to buy a home, or be in a good and stable position with our finances but it also allows us to obtain a loan easily should we ever need it.

However, it is so important, vital even, to establish your credit and have good credit if not for now but for your future. What is more, it is vital that you do fix your bad credit. What can you personally do?

1. Build Up Your Credit Slowly

The first thing that you need to do is to get your household bills in your name. If you really want to establish a better form of credit, change who the main bill payer on your utilities. Big utility companies send out information and bills to your home and even though it might not seem much, putting your name on your bills is important. If your partner has a good credit already established, ask to change them to yours.

You can actually build your credit by simply having the utility bills in your name and paying them on time every month! Yes, it is that simple, though of course, things aren't going to change overnight, it takes time but even slow progress is worth a lot.

2. Make Sure That You Pay All Of Your Bills On Time

An important part of establishing your good credit is to ensure you keep paying those bills. Try to avoid late payments; if you have to, set up reminders when the payment is due and if you can, avoid underpaying – that is worse than paying late because companies may choose not to accept anything less than full payment.

If you want to remember yourself, you could actually set up a payment system so that your bills come out of your account automatically. This can be a really great way of building your credit of paying history and help to avoid missing payments as well.

For some bills, such as your credit cards, you should try to pay at least the minimum amount each month. If you have extra money, put it towards your credit cards, however, if you are struggling, pay the minimum at least. This way you avoid a late payment and avoid adding more interest.

3. Don't Ever Go Over Your Credit Card Balance

Try to avoid going over your balance on each credit cards. You don't want to max out on your cards; it might not look too great on your credit report. If potential loan companies see you have maxed out several high balance credit cards, they might decide you are not worth the risk. Instead, try to pay at least half of the balance off before adding any more balance to it.

This will help you to avoid going over your limit and helps to keep bad credit away from you also. Of course, you can end up going over your limit on some months but if you do, try to repay the amount back as quickly as possible to keep the credit effect low. You could even get a store card from a certain store you shop at often. It could be an electrical store or food store, but whatever it may be, make sure you use it. You put a balance on the card; you repay it back at the end of the month.

4. Have A Savings Account

If you can set up a new savings account. This never hurts especially when it comes to showing potential lenders that you have a few accounts with your bank open. Even if you only add a few dollars each week, it still can look good on your part.

What is more, if you have a savings or even a checking account, your bank may be willing to offer a credit card in the future. However, don't open four or five accounts just to build credit, that doesn't look good, it's really bad so just open one savings account.

While having bad credit is bad enough, there are certain things that you can do to help yourself build up good credit while you are trying to fix it. Doing simple things such as paying all of your bills on time, not going over the balance on your credit cards and opening up a savings account can go a long way in helping you to repair your credit to a rating that not only creditors will find satisfying, but that you will find it satisfying as well.

Conclusion

Thank you very much again for downloading this book!

I really do hope that this book will help give you a better understand about credit ratings and the true importance of yours. I also hope that you learn a few proven tactics to help improve your credit score before it has a chance to get worse or fix it in the case it is already damaged.

So, what is next for you? The next step is to begin applying what you have learned in this eBook in your current situation and working as hard as you can to begin repairing your credit. What have you got to lose?

If you enjoyed this book, please do not hesitate to take the time to share your thoughts and post an honest review for me online. I would greatly appreciate it.

About Us

The Thought Flame is committed to add value to its customers through various books, online courses and other resources. You can learn more about us and our books at www.thethoughtflame.com.

Don't forget to check out our amazing **online video courses** at www.thethoughtflame.com/courses/ to take your knowledge to another level.

To check out our **extraordinary collection of diet/cookbooks**, visit http://www.thethoughtflame.com/category/non-fictional/cookbooks/ .

As a part of our valued relationship with our customers, we keep providing you free promotional books, courses and other stuff on subscribing with us on our site. We have a strict anti-spam policy and assure you no spam mails will be sent to your mailbox.

To subscribe with us, visit www.thethoughtflame.com.

Like our work and would like to say thanks? Buy us a cup of coffee at www.thethoughtflame.com/coffee/

Author

Amarpreet Singh is an avid learner and his passion for education has made him travel, work and study all across the world. He holds three masters degrees, including MBA, from top universities in Asia.

He is author of dozens of books, many of which are Amazon's bestseller, varying in various topics and categories. He also teaches many online courses having thousands of students across the world.

He has a keen interest in international affairs, economics, global poverty and politics, financial markets and entrepreneurship, and strives to be part of a community that shares the same passion.

He has worked as consultant with organizations like Airbus and The World Bank.

He loves travelling and learning about new cultures, and has been fortunate to live/work/travel/study in countries like India, China, Korea, US, South Africa, Japan, Philippines, Singapore, Canada etc., and learn about the culture and lifestyle in each of them.

To check out more of his work, visit

www.thethoughtflame.com

www.ingramcontent.com/pod-product-compliance
Lightning Source LLC
Chambersburg PA
CBHW030704190526
45164CB00004B/439